Funeral Director and Mortuary Exam Study Guide

Becoming Licensed as a Funeral Director or Embalmer

BECOMING LICENSED

There are three paths to becoming a licensed funeral director/embalmer. The first two paths require a person to go through a provisional licensing program. This program allows an individual to get practical experience under the direct and personal supervision of a licensed funeral director/embalmer. The third path is to reciprocate an active license from another state.

All licensed funeral directors/embalmers must meet the following requirements:

1. Be at least 18 years of age
2. Graduated from an accredited high school or passed GED
3. Graduated from an accredited school or college of mortuary science
4. Successfully completed the provisional licensing program (unless reciprocating from another state)
5. Successfully completed the National Board Exams and the Mortuary Law Exam (passing grade of 75%)

PROVISIONAL LICENSE PROGRAM

State law and Commission rule require Provisional License Applicants to meet the following guidelines:

1. Be at least 18 years of age
2. Have graduated or be enrolled in an accredited school or college of mortuary science (*see below)
3. Be employed during the *entirety* of the program by a funeral director/embalmer under the direct instruction and supervision of the FDIC/EIC
4. Submit to a FBI Background check

5. Successfully pass the Mortuary Law Exam prior to licensure
6. Comply with the requirements of Tex. Occ. Code, Chapter 651 and the Rules of the Commission

*A person who is not and has never been enrolled in an accredited school or college of mortuary science may receive a provisional license for a period of 12 months. However, the license will not be renewed until the licensee shows he/she is enrolled in an accredited school or college of mortuary science.

An applicant who wishes to be both a funeral director and an embalmer must submit both applications. The provisional license issued will indicate if the person is in the Funeral Director or Embalmer program. A provisional licensee who is in both programs will receive two licenses.

Path to Licensure by Exiting Directly from the Provisional Program:

In order to exit the provisional program to full licensure, a provisional licensee must submit the Provisional Exit Checklist which affirms the licensee has provided the Commission the following:

1. Certified transcript from accredited mortuary school or college that shows the degree awarded with the date conferred
2. Certificate from International Conference of Funeral Examining Boards providing National/State Board Examination score(s) of 75% or better
3. Mortuary Law Exam with score of 75% or better
4. Provisional Licensee Reporting Form(s) showing 45 completed cases signed by supervisor and FDIC/EIC

Until all administrative paperwork is returned and reviewed by the Commission, licensees REMAIN on provisional status.

Path to Licensure by NOT exiting directly from the Provisional Program

If a person is not able to exit directly from the provisional program to full licensure, the person has the option to complete the education or testing requirements while unlicensed. As the person is not licensed, the person may NOT perform acts of funeral directing or embalming. All case work must be completed during the period while the person was licensed as a provisional licensee by the Commission.

Once the person has met the requirements listed at the top of the page, the person may complete an application, re-take and pass the State Mortuary Law Exam and submit to a criminal background check. The person must have held a provisional license no more than 24 months prior to application.

The application will require the person to submit the following information:

1. Certified transcript from accredited mortuary school or college that shows the degree awarded with the date conferred
2. Certificate from International Conference of Funeral Examining Boards providing National/State Board Examination score(s) of 75% or better
3. Provisional Licensee Reporting Form showing 45 completed cases (last case no more than 24 months old) signed by supervisor and FDIC/EIC

RECIPROCAL LICENSE PROGRAM

A person can become a licensed Funeral Director and Embalmer through a reciprocal licensing program where individuals licensed in good standing in another state can be awarded a Funeral Director's and/or Embalmer's license. For those states with substantially similar licensing requirements, the applicant would need to have been licensed by that state for a minimum of one year. For those states that do not have similar licensing requirements, the applicant would need to have been licensed by that state for a minimum of five years.

Applicants must complete the application packet, successfully pass the Mortuary Law Exam and submit to a FBI Background check.

MILITARY LICENSING

If you are a member of the military, former member of the military or the spouse of a member of the military, please contact your state's licensing board for expedited licensing requirements.

ARTS

1. A joint family is always:

A. mobile

B. egalitarian

C. patriarchal

D. matriarchal

2. A funeral rite that is adjusted to the needs and wants of those involved is known as:

A. adaptive

B. humanistic

C. traditional

D. a memorial service

3. Social customs which may be broken without serious consequences are known as:

A. laws

B. norms

C. mores

D. folkways

4. The religion of the United States is basically

A. Buddhist.

B. Judeo-Christian.

C. Muslim.

D. Hindu.

5. In the late 19th century, funeral services were usually held in the
A. home.
B. funeral home.
C. city hall.
D. church building.

6. All of the following are a part of the normal grief response except:
A. guilt
B. hallucinations
C. somatic distress
D. experience symptoms of the deceased's last illness

7. Blame directed inward is the definition of:
A. guilt
B. anger
C. denial
D. dependency

8. The third stage of anticipatory grief described by Kubler-Ross is
A. anger.
B. bargaining.
C. denial.
D. depression.

9. Which of the following types of death would allow for anticipatory grief to occur?

A. SIDS

B. AIDS

C. suicide

D. homicide

10. What type of damages pay over and above the actual loss?

A. token

B. nominal

C. punitive

D. compensatory

11. Rules and Regulations passed by the Federal Trade Commission (FTC) are examples of

A. statutory law.

B. administrative law.

C. case law.

D. common law.

12. False statements made in writing for the purpose of injuring the reputation of another constitute

A. slander.

B. libel.

C. breach of character.

D. implicit trespass.

14. A contract in which terms have NOT been fully performed by all parties is

A. unexecuted.

B. unilateral.

C. illegal.

D. executory.

15. A funeral director leasing a funeral coach from a livery service is an example of what type of bailment?

A. mutual benefit

B. special

C. gratuitous

D. constructive

16. Clothes and jewelry given to the funeral director to be placed on the dead body are considered in law as

A. no property.

B. quasi-property.

C. bailed property.

D. unclaimed property.

17. Funeral claims against the decedent's estate are

A. secondary claims.

B. preferred claims.

C. illegal when filed.

D. treated as any other debt.

18. A funeral director is generally NOT responsible for accidents that occur

A. during the funeral home visitation or service.

B. at a religious facility used for the funeral.

C. at the cemetery.

D. at the place where death occurs.

19. In a cortege, drivers that are under the control of the funeral director are legally referred to as

A. agent drivers.

B. livery drivers.

C. contract drivers.

D. volunteer drivers.

20. A funeral director may discuss information on a death certificate ONLY with

A. immediate family members.

B. friends of the deceased.

21. The proper title for an officiates of the Christian Science faith is a
A. pastor.
B. priest.
C. reader.
D. speaker.

22. A Greek orthodox religious picture is called
A. a kever.
B. an icon.
C. a solea.
D. a trisagion.

23. Which of the following in NOT specifically required by the Federal Trade Commission (FTC)?
A. Casket Price List
B. Outer Burial Container Price List
C. Funeral Agreement Form
D. General Price List

24. The time limit for making application for a veteran's headstone for a deceased veteran is
A. 90 days.
B. 6 months.
C. 1 year.
D. no time limit.

25. Traditionally, the name given to a symbolic cloth covering placed over the casket is
A. a pall.
B. a veil.
C. a cape.
D. an interment cover.

26. In casket manufacturing, kapok is used as
A. a lining material.
B. a padding material.
C. a casket covering material.
D. a backing material.

27. Support from the funeral director is most recognizable in what type of selection room approach?
A. direct
B. indirect
C. private
D. nonverbal

28. A wedge-shaped burial container, which is broader at the shoulders than at the head or feet, is a
A. casket.
B. cenotaph.
C. coffin.
D. domet.

29. The part of the casket handle which the pallbearers grasp is the

A. lug.

B. arm.

C. bar.

D. ear.

30. What casket lining material is considered the standard for expensive caskets?

A. velvet

B. twill

C. crepe

31. A liquidity ratio that measures the ability of a firm to meet its current debt on short notice is called the

A. quick asset ratio.

B. debt-to-owners' equity ratio.

C. total assets ratio.

D. return-on-equity ratio.

32. Gross sales minus sales returns and allowances, and minus discounts on sales yields, are

A. total purchases.

B. operating expenses.

C. gross profit.

D. net sales.

33. A transaction in which caskets are bought on account from a supplier should be recorded as a credit to

A. sales.

B. cash.

C. accounts payable.

D. accounts receivable.

34. The right-hand amount column of a standard two-column ledger account form is called the

A. profit column.

B. loss column.

C. credit column.

D. debit column.

35. Assets that are easily converted into cash are termed

A. fixed.

B. liquid.

C. accrued.

D. intangible.

36. If the total of expenses is smaller than the total of revenues, the difference is termed

A. net worth.

B. gross profit.

C. gross margin.

D. net profit.

37. What is the interest on a $1000 note for 1 month at 8% annual interest rate?
A. $5.33
B. $5.95
C. $6.33
D. $6.67

38. When cash is spent in the acquisition of an asset, the net worth of the business is
A. not affected.
B. increased.
C. decreased.
D. balanced.

39. An increase in proprietorship as a result of a business transaction is considered
A. an asset.
B. a liability.
C. net worth.
D. income.

40. The left side of a standard account is called the
A. credit side.
B. debit side.
C. profit side.
D. balance side.

SCIENCE

1. A factor that indicates the use of a MORE dilute arterial solution is
A. thick skin.
B. tough skin.
C. emaciation.

2. In a case involving death from uremia,
A. there is muscular degeneration.
B. the ammonia reacts with formaldehyde.
C. there is vascular obstruction.
D. urine is excreted.

3. Rigor mortis and algor mortis are similar in that both are
A. before death.
B. forms of edema.
C. stiffened conditions.
D. postmortem conditions

4. How many ounces of 32-index fluid are needed to make 2 gallons of a 2% fluid dilution?
A. 8
B. 12
C. 14
D. 16

5. The settling of the blood to dependent portions of the body is called
A. livor mortis.
B. cadaveric lividity.
C. hypostasis.
D. imbibition.

6. The direction of eyebrow hair growth is laterally
A. upward.
B. upward and inward.
C. upward and outward.
D. downward and outward.

7. The width of the nose at its base is equal to the width of the
A. eye.
B. mouth.
C. eyebrow.
D. ear.

8. Which of the following sutures would best be employed for an abdominal puncture wound?
A. lock
B. baseball
C. intradermal
D. purse string

9. In posing the eyes, the eyelids should meet at the
A. center of the orbit.
B. superior third of the orbit.
C. inferior third of the orbit.
D. middle third of the orbit.

10. Hypodermic tissue building may be performed as a post embalming treatment for
A. emaciation.
B. tissue swelling.
C. controlling purge.
D. body fluid accumulation.

11. Bacteria that can grow in the absence or presence of free oxygen are known as
A. aerobes.
B. facultative.
C. obligate aerobes.
D. obligate anaerobes.

12. Which superficial dermatomycosis increases when associated with AIDS?
A. candidiasis
B. cryptococcosis
C. histoplasmosis
D. coccidioidomycosis

13. An important factor in any consideration of the mode of action of antimicrobial compounds is
A. transposition.
B. cross resistance.
C. selective toxicity.
D. plasmid-mediated resistance.

14. Pathogenic microbes are most virulent
A. after the first 24 hours.
B. during thermal death time.
C. only in the presence of dry heat.
D. when first emitted from the body.

15. Wearing protective clothing and exercising Universal Precautions while removing the deceased from the place of death

I. provides an effective barrier to portals of entry.
II. Eliminates the virulence of pathogens.
III. Reduces the number of microorganisms present.
IV. Is required by OSHA's blood borne pathogen rule.

A. I and II only
B. I and IV only

16. Which of the following is the first in the organs to decompose?
A. urinary bladder
B. lining of trachea.
C. no pregnant uterus
D. mesentery and omentum

17. A benign neoplasm found in blood vessels is a
A. hemangiosarcoma.
B. lymphangioma.
C. hemangioma.
D. leiomyoma.

18. Inflammation of the sac surrounding the heart is called
A. myocarditis.
B. pancreatitis.
C. endocarditis.
D. pericarditis.

19. Which of the following frequently results from long-term, uncontrolled diabetes mellitus?
A. erysipeias
B. gastroenteritis
C. atherosclerosis
D. Alzheimer's disease

20. Which of the following conditions would be caused by a thrombus as evidenced during embalming?

I. diminished distribution
II. edema
III. intravascular resistance
IV. atrophy

A. I and II only
B. I and III only
C. II and IV only
D. III and IV only

21. Extremely hard water should NOT be used in diluting embalming fluid because it
A. causes dehydration.
B. prevents oxidation.
C. results in blood coagulation.
D. prevents permeation of the fluids.

22. Chemicals that have the capability of displacing unpleasant odors are
A. humectants.
B. deodorants.
C. surfactants.
D. disinfectants.

23. Which of the following is characteristic of a jaundice fluid?
A. no bleach content
B. no counter staining
C. low formaldehyde content
D. high formaldehyde content

24. To facilitate the penetration of preservatives during surface embalming, the surface gels may contain
A. phenol.
B. sodium citrate.
C. sodium lauryl sulfate.
D. quaternary ammonium compounds.

25. The recommended initial 3% dilution of a 20-Index standard arterial chemical used to embalm an edematous body would be which of the following?
A. 3 oz. of arterial to 125 oz. of water
B. 5 oz. of arterial to 123 oz. of water
C. 16 oz. of arterial to 112 oz. of water
D. 19 oz. of arterial to 109 oz. of water

26. Which of the following lists the vessels in order going from the aorta towards the upper extremity?

I. axillary
II. brachiocephalic
III. brachial
IV. subclavian

A. I, II, III, IV
B. II, III, I, IV
C. II, IV, I, III
D. III, IV, I, II

27. The external iliac artery lies along the medial border of which of the following muscles?
A. psoas major
B. coracobrachialis
C. pectoralis major
D. external oblique

28. In relation to the lungs, the heart is
A. medial.
B. lateral.
C. inferior.
D. superior.

29. Blood flow to the arm and hand will reach the following arteries in what order?

I. brachial
II. axillary
III. radial
IV. deep palmar arch

A. I, II, III, IV
B. II, I, III, IV
C. III, IV, I, II
D. IV, I, III, II

30. When using the 9-region method for cavity embalming, the cecum is located in which of the following regions?
A. hypogastric
B. right lumbar
C. left inguinal
D. right inguinal

1. A will is an instrument for the ordered disposition of real and personal property that is to take effect upon death. Which of the following is a requirement for a will to take effect?

- ○ Both "The deceased was of legal age": and "There was intestacy on the part of the legatee":

- ○ There was intestacy on the part of the legatee

- ○ The will has a codicil

- ○ **The deceased was of legal age**

2. **The Funeral Rule, which is enforced by the Federal Trade Commission (FTC), has many provisions. These include mandated disclosures and restrictive actions. At the very start of a face-to-face discussion with the public regarding the selection of funeral goods or services and/or the prices of them, the funeral director is required to give the consumer:**

- ○ The GPL for retention upon collection and signed receipt of the Consumer Protection Fee

- ○ The casket price list and vault price list for retention, and the GPL for reference only

- ○ The price for each item the consumer requests on dated company letterhead

- ○ **The GPL for retention, and the casket and vault price list for reference only**

3. **The person with the authority and duty of final disposition who may or may not have "actual" custody (physical possession) of the deceased at a particular moment is considered to have what kind of custody?**

- ○ Consignment

- ○ Caveat emptor

- ○ **Constructive**

- ○ Endowment

4. An insolvent estate is an estate of a deceased person whose assets are insufficient to pay the estate's debts, taxes, and administrative expenses. It is the state statute that controls the priority of these claims. In most states, though, the priority of claims—from top priority to lowest—is ordered as follows:

- ○ Taxes, funeral expenses, and medical bills

- ○ **Funeral expenses, administration expenses, and taxes**

- ○ Medical bills, taxes, and funeral expenses

- ○ Administration expenses, funeral expenses, and taxes

5. A federal government agency created to promote consumer protection, encourage free and fair competition, and prevent what regulators determine to be anti-competitive business practices is called:

- ○ ICCFA

- ○ **FTC**

- ○ OSHA

- ○ NFDA

6. A wrongful act by a person for which damages can be sought by the injured party through a civil lawsuit is called a:

- ○ Mutilation

- ○ Replevin

- ○ Obstruction

- ○ **Tort**

7. The power of a government to impose what it considers reasonable restrictions and laws on its citizens for the maintenance of public safety, health, order, and welfare is called:

- ○ Uniform probate code

- ○ Restrictive covenant

- ○ Tort

- ○ **Police power**

8. **Which of the following funeral rites is conducted without the presence of the casketed body?**

- ○ Traditional or complete cremation service

- ○ Graveside service

- ○ **Memorial service**

- ○ Entombment service

9. A deceased veteran or reservist who was entitled to receive retired military pay qualifies to receive an American flag after the completion and submittal of the APPLICATION FOR UNITED STATES FLAG FOR BURIAL PURPOSES form, also known as:

- ○ VA form 40-1330

- ○ VA Form 21-530

- ○ SSA-721

- ○ **VA form 90-2008**

10. A portable stretcher used by both ambulances and funeral homes to move the injured or deceased that is considered to be the most important item for transferring remains from a house or an institution is called a:

- ○ **Cot**

- ○ Flexible stretcher

- ○ Transfer vehicle

- ○ Church truck

11.   Which of the following accurately describe the purposes of a death certificate?
i. Shows vital statistics and cause of death for medical or actuarial research
ii. Is the legal permanent record of the deceased
iii. Is the legal document issued by the proper government agency authorizing the transportation and/or disposition of human remains
iv. Is the legal record that final disposition has occurred

- ○ All of the above

- ○ i and ii

- ○ ii and iv

- ○ i , ii, and iv

12.   A typical funeral cortege would be arranged in the following order:

- ○ Lead car, hearse, clergy, pallbearers, family cars/limo, and procession

- ○ Hearse, lead car, clergy, pallbearers, family cars/limo, and procession

- ○ Lead car, hearse, pallbearers, clergy, family cars/limo, and procession

- ○ **Lead car, clergy, pallbearers, hearse, family cars/limo, and procession**

13. The entryway, foyer, or lobby to a funeral home or church is also called the:

- ○ Nave

- ○ Niche

- ○ **Narthex**

- ○ Sanctuary

14. In the Roman Catholic faith, an anointing ceremony by a priest for the seriously ill to bring healing or for those who are dying to prepare their souls for eternity is called:

- ○ Rosary Beads

- ○ Rosary Service

- ○ Paschal Candle Service

- ○ **Sacrament of the Sick**

15. The name for the sanctified elements of Holy Communion that comprise the essential rudiments for liturgical worship is:

- ○ Trisagion

- ○ Paschal Candle

- ○ **Eucharist**

- ○ Communion Paten

1. The Centers for Disease Control concluded that funeral directors had an elevated risk of contracting a variety of blood borne and airborne pathogens as a result of their contact with dead human bodies, and found that the most frequently reported diseases by funeral directors included:

a. Hematoma
b. Staphylococcal infection
c. Cutaneous tuberculosis
d. Both b and c

Answer Key

d: Both b and c:

The Centers for Disease Control (CDC) has determined through studies conducted with practicing funeral directors that the most common blood borne and airborne pathogens contracted through exposure to dead human bodies are staphylococcal infections and cutaneous (skin) tuberculosis. A staphylococcal infection is a very contagious malady that can be transmitted from person to person from droplets from the nose of an infected person or from the bacteria in the pus oozing out of an infected lesion. Cutaneous tuberculosis (TB) is tuberculosis on the skin caused by the mycobacterium tuberculosis, and if the embalmer is exposed to this a skin infection called tuberculosis chancre may occur. A hematoma is due to a leaking blood vessel, and results in an area with a collected pool of blood.

2. The ventilation of a prep room is measured using the number of air exchanges per hour. This is calculated by taking the total square footage of the room and then determining the size of the air handler or fan needed to move the air out and replace it in a given amount of time. According to Robert Mayer author of Embalming: History, Theory & Practice; the air exchange rate for a preparation room should be between _____ and _____ per hour.

a. 5 - 8
b. 5 - 10
c. 20 - 30
d. 12 - 20

2. d: 12 - 20. Air exchanges per hour refers to the movement of a volume of air in a given period of time. According to the Mortuary College textbook Embalming: History, Theory & Practice by Robert Mayer, the exchange rate should be between 12 and 20 exchanges per hour for ventilation to be considered adequate. Air exchange rates of between 5 - 8 or 5-10 exchanges per hour are not adequate. Air exchange rates of 20 - 30 per hour are higher than necessary.

3. There are approximately six devices that can be used to inject arterial solution. Which of the following is NOT a device historically used during embalming?

a. Bulb syringe
b. Gravity bottle
c. Centrifugal pump
d. Hand pump

3. C: Centrifugal pump. The centrifugal pump is a relatively contemporary device compared to all the other choices because it uses an electric pump to produce pressure that can be delivered with or without a pulsating effect. The bulb syringe was a device that was used in the past in embalming. It was manually squeezed to deliver and release pressure and the ensuing flow. The gravity bottle was a frequently used historic technique of embalming that used the force of gravity to move embalming fluids. The hand pump was another device historically used for embalming that relied on the manual action of one's hand to create pressure and move fluid.

4. Another term used to describe the front, or anterior, of the body is:

a. Dorsal
b. Anatomical position
c. Medial
d. Ventral

4. d: Ventral. Ventral is an anatomical expression used to refer to the anterior or frontal portion of the human body. Dorsal is an anatomical phrase used to describe the posterior or rear of the human body. Anatomical position is the recognized scientific standard of how a human body should be situated so that all directions and positions are determined in the same way. Medial refers to the midline area (medial plane) of the human body.

5. A type of suture used to close incisions so that the ligature remains entirely under the epidermis is called:

a. Basket weave suture
b. Intradermal suture
c. Bridge stitch
d. Loop stitch

5. b: Intradermal suture. The intradermal suture (hidden suture) is used to secure incisions so the ligature remains concealed under the skin. The basket weave suture (cross stitch) is a system of stitches that crosses the limits of an excision to secure fillers and hold tissues in their proper positions. The bridge stitch (interrupted suture) is a short-term suture made up of divided pieces that are tied to hold the tissue in its proper position. They are removed later. The loop stitch is a single stitch used to secure restorative materials.

1. The grieving and adaptation to living after the loss of a loved one is called:

    A. Mourning
    B. Bereavement
    C. Thanatology

2. There are three main factors that influence the grieving process. They are psychological, sociological, and:

    A. External
    B. Internal
    C. Physiological

3. If a woman deposits money in a preneed burial account at her local bank, the bank assumes which of the following roles?

    A. Assignee
    B. Devisee
    C. Fiduciary

4. A trial balance will help a business owner do which of the following?

    A. Keep track of inventory
    B. Help with vehicle maintenance
    C. Show profits and losses
    D. Ensure accurate payroll

5. A suture made around a circular opening or puncture that closes the margins when it is pulled is called a:

    A. Basket weave suture
    B. Purse suture
    C. Bridge suture
    D. Whip suture

6. The molecular movement of matter from an area of greater concentration to an area of lower concentration is:

    A. Hydrolysis
    B. Saturation
    C. Diffusion
    D. Compound

7. Autopsies can be done on the complete torso and cranium, and on which of the following?

    A. Thorax
    B. Arms
    C. Legs
    D. Neck

8. The CDC lists at least nine hazardous body fluids. Which of the following is one of them?

    A. Urine
    B. Saliva
    C. Spinal fluid
    D. Perspiration

9. There are three types of blood vessels: arteries, veins, and:

    A. Atria
    B. Ventricles
    C. Valves
    D. Capillaries

Flashcards Terms

Animalistic View

Early roman view of the afterlife where soul would hover around place of burial and required constant attention to be happy. Neglect would bring evil upon family

Babylonians

Culture associated with the practice of immersing the body of the dead in earthen jars filled with honey and wax

Barber- Surgeon

1540-1745 sole agency permitted to embalm and perform anatomical dissection in the city of London

Bloodletting

Belief/practice of draining a quantity of blood to cure illness or disease

Burial case

Beneric American term for all burial receptacles

Burial Club

1800's London: cost of funerals were shared by others via weekly collections: forerunners of insurance

Burial in Woolen Act 1666

Required woolen cloths instead of linen, an attempt to shift imported linin to paper industry and supply customers for wool

Casket

Meaning jewel box: a ridged container designed to encase human remains

Catacombs

Roman Origin: excavated cemeteries out of rock for the tombs of wealthy Christians

Catafalque

Raised platform used for a body to lie in state

Chadwick Report

1840s reporting unsanitary conditions in London due to intramural burials, high cost of funerals and the 1st use of death certificates

Edwin Chadwich

Investigated mass corruption in regards to English burial practices who recommended that cemeteries be municipalized and religious rites be simplified

Circle if necessity

Egyptian culture, the journey to the Sun and back which required 3000 years to complete

Coffin

Utilitarian container used to hold human remains: often anthropoidal

Cooling Board

Portable table where bodies were placed while corpse cooler was in use: later became home embalming tables

Corpse Cooler

Type of ice chest placed over the torso in order to slow the process of decomposition, undertaker was responsible for the ice

Cortege

Funeral procession

Cremation

Disposition by fire: attributed to the Greeks

Crier

Middle Ages custom of a person walking the street calling out the name of the deceased and asking people to pray for their soul

Designator

M.C. and director of ancient roman funerals

Drummer

Traveling salesmen who went from town to town selling their products to early embalmers

Effigy

Life-size waxen recreation of the deceased.....used in place of deceased when body could not be preserved for long periods of time

Elysian Fields

Greek version of heaven

Extramural burial

Burial outside the walls of the city introduced during Roman times

Funeralis

Latin for torchlight procession

Funeral undertaker

Organized and facilitated funeral

Furnishing undertaker

Provided supplies and mech. to funeral undertakers (middle man)

Jean Gannal

French chemist who developed injection embalming through carotid artery

J. Anthony Gaussardia

Patented a process of embalming involving injecting an arsenic-alcohol mixture

Gravity injector

Apparatus used to inject arterial fluid that relies on gravity to create pressure (0.45 lbs per foot of elevation)

Hand pump

Method to apply continuous flow of embalming solution via hand held mechanism

Dr. William Harvey

Discovered the circulation of blood

Dr. Thomas Holmes

Father of MODERN embalming in the U.S

August Hoffman

Discovered formaldehyde

Inviter to funerals

Called personally upon those expected to attend funerals, was a municipal appointment

Layers out of the dead

Occupation specifically in many larger US cities in the late 18th c. predecessor to the undertaker

League of Prayers

Formed in Middle Ages by lay persons to bury the dead and to pray for the souls of the faithful departed

Anton von Leeuwenhock

Inventor of the microscope

"Father of microbiology"

Libitina

Ancient Roman goddess of corpse and funerals

Libitinarius

Undertaker in ancient Rome, secular role model for today's funeral director, conducted business at the temple of Libitina where death was also registered

Life signals

Made with devices to signal if someone was buried alive

Marcello Malphighi

Father of histology

Study of tissue

Mound burial

Ancient Viking custom of placing deceased in their boat and cremating, then burying with dirt

Mystery cults

Religion emphasizing spiritual aspects of the afterlife and the hope to join the cult god in a wonderful existence in eternity

Natron

A salt used by ancient Egyptians in the mummification process

Necropolis

Egyptian walled suburban city where embalming was performed also called city of the dead

Obsequies

Historic term for funeral ceremonies

Ogee design

Innovation introduced to square sided caskets to reduce excess weight and space

Osiris

Egyptian god of the underworld and judge of the dead

Pagan

Person who has no religion and enjoys the delights of sensual pleasures

Pollinctores

Name of the ancient roman embalmers (either slaves or employees of Libitinarius)

Pracco

Aka crier, summoned participants to Roman funerals

Professional mourners

Hired women to mourn, shriek and show adequate emotion for the dead

Purgatorial doctrine

Catholic belief that those whose souls are not perfectly cleansed undergo a process of cleaning before entering heaven

Dr. Auguste Renourd

Author of the undertaker's manual: first embalming book published in the US

Fredrick Ruysch

Father of embalming, first to refine arterial injection into vascular system

Sarcophagus

Cut coffin out of massive stone (Egyptian)

Sexton

Church caretaker who was responsible for digging graves

Soul shot

Mortuary fee paid to ensure entrance of the soul into heaven

Trade embalmer

Has no single employer, embalms for funeral home that have no embalmer

Undertaker

Occupation which includes responsibilities to organized and facilitate funeral activities (funeral director)

New York funeral directors exam

1. Funeral directing advisory board PBH ARTICLE 34 sec.3402

Has 10 members, 3 represent the consumer interest, 6 are license directors and 1 must be an officer, director or employee of a cemetery corporation.

3 yr. term, chairman and vice chair elected yearly, members receive no compensation, directors must be licensed at least 5 yr.

2. Funeral directing fees, fines an penalties article 34 sec.3403

Shall be paid to the dept., licensing and registration fees are deposited into a misc. special revenue fund 339.

3. Requirements for funeral directing license and practice article 34 sec. 3404

Pass funeral directing exam, citizen of U.S. or lawful alien admitted for permanent residency, obtain mortuary degree, register with dept. of health and pay registration fee $50.
Pass national exam, complete 1 yr. as resident, then pass state exam.

4. Funeral directing exams and content

Commissioner chooses content, exam given twice annually, three attempts allowed within a3 yr. period after training

5. License requirements to practice article 34 sec. 3423

Reexaminations are allowed for those who fail, for a fee of $5, once you pass pay $10 you get the license. If you are in the military and your active status interrupts your training, you have 1 year after date of discharge to resume training.

6. Funeral directing trainee reporting article34 sec. 3424

Keep file of periodic records to submit to department quarterly, notify dept. promptly of any changes in registration or employment.

7. Licensing and reciprocity with other states article 34 sec.3426

You may obtain a license in another state without taking an exam by paying a $300 fee and submission of satisfactory qualification:
a. requirements from prior state equivalent to the new state.

b. similar recognition
c. must have been engaged in funeral directing with license for 3 years or more in one or more states.
d. actually engaged in the practice at the time of application and in good standing.

8. Issuance of duplicate licenses article 34 sec.3427

Once proof has been given of lost or damaged license, a duplicate will be issued for a fee of $20.

9. Registration and licensing fees
article 34 sec. 3428

1) a. Biennial (every 2 years) application is required of funeral directors for renewal of certificate of registration; and submit a report of facts requested by DOH.
b. Report must contain names, addresses and title of all officers and directors not excluding stockholders names and addresses who own no less than 10% interest.

c. It must also include if any of the above mentioned have been convicted of a crime 2 years prior to date of application.

c1. The crime must be listed and where it occurred along with the disposition of the crime.

d. Report must list any violations of statues that the above mentioned may have been found guilty of and list statute.

e. DOH must immediately be notified by written statement of conviction of any of its officers.

f. DOH must be notified of sale or transfer of all assets or termination of business or sale or transfer of controlling interest.

f1. Must include names of transferee and transfer-er. This must occur no less than 10 days after sale or transfer or not less than 30 days prior to end of operation of business.

2) a. Biennial registration fee $62.50 (for undertakers and embalmers only)
b. $125 biennial registration fee for Funeral Directors but there is no initial registration fee.
c. Only a registered funeral firm may operate, practice, etc., a funeral firm. If a firm conducts business from more than one establishment it must be registered for each establishment. If more than one firm operates from one establishment each firm must have its own registration. Each is required to pay a registration fee of $400 for the period ending with the current biennial registration; the biennial registration is $300.
d. Funeral firm owners must pay a $100 registration fee for the amendment of a certificate of registration indicating: location, change of manager, firm name, etc.
e. Failure to register additional fee of $10 for each day after 30 days or beyond biennial registration which shall be added to the fee.

10.   Continuing education
article 34 sec.3429

1. Definitions of terms
a.) Biennium - any two year period
b.) Continuing education - course of instruction in the field of funeral directing
c.) Contact hour - period of 50-60 minutes continuously measured
d.) Provider - national, state or local trade association of funeral directors
e.) Trade association - organization which has been organized and maintained for at least 2 years prior to offering continuing education.
2. Requirement
a.) Every person shall file with the department along with biennial application a certificate attesting to the completion of courses of instruction.

b.) certification form shall include: full name and registration number, statement attesting to your attendance of specified number of hours of continuing education, signature and date.

c.)This does not apply to inactive directors

3. Minimum hours are as follows: 12 hours within each biennium, including at least 2 hours relating to state law, embalming, funeral

directing and pre need services.

5. Subjects of continuing education: aftercare, business administration, religion, natural science, etc.

6. Credit for prep. : A FD can prepare to teach an hour of continuing education and receive a 2 hour credit after he/ she teaches said class. But no more. Than 6 hours per biennium can be earned this way.

7. Class room time: 50% in a live classroom the remainder can be in the form of: video, audio, teleconference, satellite seminars, internet, and credits for preparation or correspondence work.

8. Licensees in other states: a non-resident may be granted licensee credit for continuing education

9. Late filling:

A.) a fine equal to the biennial registration for the first lateness, with a grace period of 120 days into the biennium. After 120 days registration will be suspended for the remainder of the biennium.

B.) Second violation will have and additional one of no more than $500 and suspension

C.) Inactive registrations can be reinstated by completing 12 hours of continuing education effort you get reinstated.

D.) Suspensions due to violation of filling requirement shall be reinstated by paying a fee of $500 and completing12 hours of continuing education.

E.) A notice will be sent by regular mail notice of suspension

11.   Sanitary code sub chapter J sec. 78.3

Customer's designation of intention :
Required for all cremations, must be filled out at time of arrangements, a copy goes to the next of kin at the time of the arrangements, complete this form when family comes to pick up cremations (at the time of disposition). Maintain a copy on file for 4 years. This form must include what will happen to unclaimed remains after 120 days. (Tomb, mausoleum crypt. niche, burial or scattering at sea etc.)

12.   Sanitary code sub chapter j sec. 78.2

The Contract: must contain:
Name, address and phone of the firm. Keep contracts in numerical order. The name of the deceased, place of death, date of death, date of arrangement, no blank line (N/A),
- it has 4 sections (funeral home charges, cash advances summary of charges and explanation of charges),
-2 limited services (forwarding remains to and receiving remains from)
-2 alternative services (Direct burial and direct cremation),

-places to order caskets, vaults, clothing
- Explanation of charges
-Disclosure: embalming, vault, etc.
- Cash advances (
cemetery/crematory,clergy,pall bearers,
certified D.C., etc.)
-signed 7 printed name of licensed funeral
director and reg #

13.   Sanitary code subchapter J sec. 79.4

- 4 disclosure statements are required to be
on the General Price list
A.) The goods and services shown below are
those we can provide to our customers

B.) This list may not include prices for certain
items that you selected such as cemetery or
crematory service charges, flowers, etc.

C.) Any funeral arrangements you select will
include a charge for our services.

D.) We charge you for our services inbuying
certain items

Study Notes

14. Each funeral home registration must have a separate telephone line.

15. Signs: Lettering in front of Funeral Home must be a minimum of 1.5 inches.
Casket Showroom lettering minimum .5 inch. Conspicuously displayed.

16. Food and Beverage: Prohibited in the Funeral Establishment

17. Must a Funeral firm display a sign outside the building? Yes. 1.5 inch minimum.

18. Can non-licensed funeral home employees have business cards? No. Only a funeral director with license can have business cards.

19.   How do New York State laws govern advertising in relation to funeral homes? 1. Sign in front with name as registered, a minimum of 1.5 inches. 2. Business cards are only for Directors
3. Must disclose if your license is inactive.

20.   In New York State, is it legal to serve food and beverages in the funeral home? No

21.   Who may execute an anatomical gift? Anyone over the age of 18 of "sound mind", next of kin, designated agent

22.   Can anatomical gifts be executed through a will? Yes

23.   Can a funeral home require that funeral bills be paid in advanced? Yes. However, this must be disclosed in your itemization statement or agreement. All customers must be treated equally.

24. Can a funeral home charge interest on an unpaid balance? If so, how much? Yes, you can charge interest. The maximum rate of interest that a funeral home can charge is 16% pursuant to the NYS banking law.

25. Can a funeral home charge back to the family a credit card surcharge? No. Must be listed as a cash advanced item.

26. What amount does New York State reimburse localities for burial of the indigent? 900 dollars.

27. Can unclaimed cadavers be delivered to schools for study? Yes, hospital director.

28. Is body stealing a felony? Yes, Class D felony

29. Is receiving a stolen body a felony too? No, receiving a stolen body is a misdemeanor

30. If the funeral holds the dead body in arrest because the bill was unpaid, is it a misdemeanor? Yes. 'You can't hold the body from family.

31. Is disturbing a funeral considered to be a misdemeanor? Yes. Disturbing a funeral is a misdemeanor.

32. If the funeral is not currently taking place, is it a misdemeanor to protest outside the funeral home? No. The funeral must not be taking place during protest.

33. What does the winter burial law do? Requires cemeteries to make interments available throughout the year, at least 6 days per week, excluding legal holidays.

34. To which cemeteries does the law apply? It applies to all not for profit cemeteries.

35.   What if bad weather will not permit an interment? The law clearly states that cemeteries would not have to perform interments or provide grave openings during severe weather.

36.   Can cemeteries still close based on specific dates/times of the year? No, a cemetery cannot close for any set period of time.

37.   What if a cemetery refuses to open to perform an interment, even if the weather would permit it? Contact the Division of Cemeteries Regional Division Office Investigator.

38.   Can a cemetery charge for a "winter burial?" Yes, they can charge "actual and reasonable" additional costs necessary for the interment. Cannot be a fixed price because it should be specific to what is needed at the time.

39.   Do hospital administrators have any duties regarding death certificates? Yes. When death occurs in hospital, person in charge shall promptly present certificate to physician.

40.   Are death certificates taxable? No

41.   Can a New York State funeral director file a death certificate in another state? No

42.   Must the attending physician sign a death certificate? No, it can also be signed by a physician acting on behalf of the attending physician. Or, a medical examiner.

43.   Can a non-licensed funeral director own a funeral home? Yes, but the firm must be a corporation or LLC. Un-licensed owned cannot engage in funeral directing.

44.   Are funeral directors allowed to serve on cemetery boards? Yes, however the law does state that they cannot be the majority of owners.

45.   Can a New York funeral
        director conduct a complete
        funeral in Jersey? No

46.   How many continuing
        education credits every 2 years?
        12 credit hours

47.   Are funeral directors allowed
        to sell pre need funeral insurance?
        No you cannot sell preneed
        funeral insurance.

Texas State Mortuary Law Exam

1. In order to supervise a provisional licensee, the sponsor mush have been licensed for a minimum of ____ years (**2 years**)

2. Texas Law requires the funeral service establishment document the efforts to obtain permission to embalm for a minimum of ____ hours (**Three**)

3. One must be a provisional licensee for a minimum of ___ months and a maximum of ___ months (**12, 24**)

4. When does 'Funeral Directing' begin? **First Call**

5. When does 'Funeral Directing' end? **Entombment, inurnment, permanent transport out of state, or other final services are complete**

6. When must the GPL/retail price list be handed to the prospective customer? **Must be physically presented before being shown merchandise**

7. When must the Consumer Information Brochure ('Facts about funerals') be given to the prospective customer? **must be presented at the same time as the retail price list/GPL**

8. The TFSC can charge penalties ranging from _____ to ___ dollars. **($100-$5000)**

9. Texas law _____ requires embalming. (**Never**)

10.   What must be given to any person upon request? (**a retail price list/GPL**)

11. Funeral Director in Charge, FDIC. (**is ultimately responsible for compliance with all mortuary, health and vital statistic laws**)

12. When must a burial transit permit accompany a body? (**when being transported by a common carrier**)

13. When is a burial transit permit NOT required? (**when being transported by a private carrier**)

14. In accordance with the TFSC, how many caskets are required to be sold? (**you must have at least five adult caskets, two of which must be full size, and one of which must be your least expensive**)

15. Your least expensive casket. (**must be full size and on display; and displayed in the same manner as other caskets**)

16. Commercial embalming establishments must (**designate and embalmer in charge**)

17. Commercial embalming establishments must not (**do business for the general public**)

18. Regardless of their use of a commercial embalming establishment, a funeral home must (**have a fully functional prep room with sufficient equipment and supplies for normal operation**)

19. Every funeral home must designate a (**Funeral director in charge**)

20. A provisional cannot complete the funeral director apprenticeship at a (**commercial embalming establishment. must completed in a funeral home.**)

21. Members of the TFSC shall serve _____ terms (**staggered six year**)

22. (sec 651.351, 353) In Texas, _____ is not required to own a funeral establishment or cemetery (**a funeral director's license (sec 651.351, 353)**)

23. Solicitation (**any direct or indirect contact a person near death or their family in attempt to influence their selection of a funeral service provider. This behavior is against the law.**)

24. There are ___ members of the TFSC (**seven (two dual licensed, one cemetery operator, four members of the general public)**)

25.   the TFSC meets (**once per quarter of every calendar year**)

26.   If you get a subpoena from the TFSC, (**you must appear for a hearing and bring any requested documents**)

27.   (sec 651.157) How often should a cemetery, crematory, funeral establishment, etc., shall be inspected by the TFSC at least (once every two years (sec 651.157))

28.   (sec 651.1571) For perpetual care cemeteries, inspection is not required unless _____ (an interment has taken place in the past two years, or the commission has received a complaint (sec 651.1571))

29.   How many hours are required to complete a provisional license? (**There is no provision in the TAC concerning hours worked for a provisional license. This is not covered by the law.**)

30.   (sec 651.261) A license holder shall _____ the holder's license in _____ place of business at which the license holder practices (**conspicuously display; each (sec 651.261)**)

31.   (sec 651.266) For continuing education, it is required to have __ hours to facilitate renewal every ___ years 16; 2 (sec 651.266)

32.   (sec 651.266) For continuing education, it is required that you have 2 hours each of (**vital stats, TX law, ethics**)

33.   (sec 651.266) for the remaining 8 hours of CEU credits, some can be gained by attending **(meetings at the TFSC (sec 651.266))**

34.   (sec 651.266) For continuing education, it is required that you have 2 hours each of (**vital stats, TX law, ethics**)

35.   (sec 651.266) for the remaining 8 hours of CEU credits, some can be gained by attending) **(meetings at the TFSC (sec 651.266)**

36.   (sec 651.306) Personal Supervision: for the purposes of this chapter, person supervision requires the _____ of a funeral director at the specified time and place a funeral service is being provided (**physical presence (sec 651.266)**)

37.   (sec 651.401) If there is no reasonable probability that a representative of the funeral home will encounter a family member [or other person by whom the arrangements will be made] then the person doing the pick-up does not have to be a _____ **(licensed funeral director or embalmer (sec 651.401))**

38.   (sec 651.401) if an unlicensed person inadvertently encounters a family member of the deceased [or the person who will be making the arrangements], the unlicensed person shall restrict communication to **(1) identifying the unlicensed person's employer 2)arrange an appointment with a licensed person 3) make any legally required disclosures)**

39.   (sec 651.401) Note: provisional MAY **(ask for permission to embalm, and MAY give out a GPL)**

40.   (sec 651.404) When funeral services are discussed, an agent of the funeral home must provide _____ with a brochure containing consumer information (each prospective customer; 'Facts about Funerals' (sec 651.404))

41.   (Sec 651.452) a person violates this chapter and may lose their license if they.... (**Commit any misdemeanor related to funeral directing or embalming, commit any felony, are deemed by a court to be of unsound mind, or become unfit to practice due to substance abuse (sec 651.452)**)

42.   (sec 651.458) a person violates chapter if they make a distinction ... (**in providing funeral information to a customer regardless of any affiliation of the customer or whether the customer has a present need for services or merchandise (sec 651.458)**)

43.   (sec 651.508) If a person violates chapter ___ of the Health and Safety code, they also violate this chapter **(716, (651))**

44.   (sec 651.651) Cremation is defined as **(the irreversible process of reducing human remains to bone fragments through direct flame, extreme heat, and evaporation. The term may include pulverization, which is the process of reducing identifiable bone fragments after cremation and processing granulated particles by manual or mechanical means.)**

45.   Crematory license (sec 651.656) **(a person may not conduct a crematory business in this state unless the person who is the owner of the crematory holds a crematory establishment license issued by the commission.)**

46.	(sec 651.656) A person may not hold a crematory establishment license unless they ... (**hold a funeral establishment license or a commercial embalming establishment license. (sec 651.656)**)

47.	(sec 651.685) Annually, each crematory must file a report to the commission. This report must include: (**the number of cremations performed the previous year**)

48.	(sec 695.001) "Casket" means (**a container used to hold the remains of a deceased person.**)

49.	(sec 695.002) The commission shall ensure that a casket ... (**contains ID of the deceased person**)

50.	(sec 695.002) in-casket identification must include (**person's name, date of birth, and date of death**)

51.   Ingress: (**a right or permission to enter**)

52.   Egress: (**a right or permission to exit**)

53.   How often does the commission update 'Facts about Funerals'? (**The commission shall review and revise the information of consumer interest prepared and disseminated by the commission on a biennial basis.**)

54.   If a person is licensed, but not practicing, how much Continuing Ed. must they have? (**they need six hours for renewal**)

Funeral Director Exam California

Study Notes:

7617 place of business licensing: The business of a licensed funeral establishment shall be conducted and engaged in at a fixed place or facility. No person, partnership, association, corporation, or other organization shall open or maintain a place or establishment at which to engage in or conduct, or hold himself or herself or itself out as engaging in or conducting, the business of a funeral establishment without a license.

7623 separate locations licensees: If an applicant for a funeral establishment license proposes to engage in or conduct more than one funeral establishment, the applicant shall make a separate application and procure a separate license for each separate establishment.

7624 one director per establishment: Not more than one person, partnership, or other organization engaged in business as a funeral establishment shall transact business in one specific funeral facility.

7628 application to change place of business: Any person, partnership, association, corporation, or other organization desiring to change the location of a licensed funeral establishment shall apply therefor on forms furnished by the bureau and shall include a fee fixed by this chapter.

7629 unfair competition: No funeral establishment shall be conducted or held forth as being conducted or advertised as being conducted under any name which misleads the public.

7630 assignment of license: A funeral establishment's license may be assigned upon payment of the fee fixed by this chapter and upon submission of an audit report prepared and signed by an independent certified public accountant or public accountant currently licensed in this state.

7631 death of a licensee: In case of the death of a licensed funeral director who leaves a funeral establishment as part or all of the assets of his or her estate, the bureau may issue a temporary license to his or her legal representative, unless the legal representative has committed crime under Section 480.

7632 embalming: A funeral director shall cause all human remains embalmed in or at the direction of his or her funeral establishment to be embalmed by a licensed embalmer, by an apprentice embalmer under the supervision of his or her licensed supervising embalmer, or by a student in a program accredited by the American Board of Funeral Service Education under the supervision of a licensed embalmer.

7633 death certificate fees: No funeral director shall charge a fee for filing a certificate of death or for providing copies thereof in excess of fees set by statute for filing and providing certified copies of such certificates.

7634 removal of tissues: Notwithstanding any other provision of law, a licensed embalmer, at the request of a licensed physician, may remove tissue from human remains for transplant, or therapeutic, or scientific purposes.

7641 unlicensed practice students and instructors: It is unlawful for any person to embalm a body, or engage in, or hold himself or herself out as engaged in practice as an embalmer, unless he or she is licensed by the bureau.

7643 applicant's qualifications: In order to qualify for a license as an embalmer, the applicant shall comply with all of the following requirements: (a) be over 18 years of age.

(b) Not have committed acts or crimes constituting grounds for denial of licensure under Section 480.

(c) Have completed at least two years of apprenticeship under an embalmer licensed and engaged in practice as an embalmer in this state in a funeral establishment (d) Have graduated from a mortuary science program approved by the bureau and accredited by the American Board of Funeral Service Education.

7648 embalmers license no assignable: No embalmer's license is assignable, and only the licensee may engage in the practice of embalming under the license.

7649 signature of licensee on certificate: Except as provided in Section 102805 of the Health and Safety Code, whenever the name of any licensed embalmer is subscribed to any certificate, the purport of which is that he or she has performed any act mentioned in the certificate, the licensed embalmer shall actually sign his or her name thereto.

7680 display of license: Every license issued shall be displayed conspicuously in the place of business or employment of the licensee. The form and content of every license issued shall be determined in accordance with Section 164.

7692 business conduct; fraud: Misrepresentation or fraud in the conduct of the business or the profession of a funeral director or embalmer constitutes a ground for disciplinary action.

7692.5 misrepresentation of burial regulations to obtain business: Any false or misleading statement regarding any law or regulation pertaining to the preparation for burial, transportation for burial, or burial of the dead, made willfully by a licensee to obtain business as a funeral director or embalmer, constitutes a ground for disciplinary action.

7693 false or misleading advertising: False or misleading advertising as a funeral establishment, funeral director, or embalmer constitutes a ground for disciplinary action.

7694 solicitation of business- advertising exception: Solicitation, after a death or while a death is impending, of funeral directing or embalming business by the licensee, or by the agents, assistants or employees of the licensee, when such solicitation is authorized or ratified by the licensee, constitutes a ground for disciplinary action.

7695 employment of cappers and solicitors: Employment by the licensee of persons known as "cappers" or "steerers" or "solicitors," or other such persons to solicit, after a death or while a death is impending, funeral directing or embalming business constitutes a ground for disciplinary action.

7696 employment of persons to solicit bodies: Employment, directly or indirectly, of any apprentice, agent, assistant, embalmer, employee or other person, on part or full time, or on commission, for the purpose of calling upon individuals or institutions by whose influence human remains may be turned over to a particular funeral director or embalmer constitutes a ground for disciplinary action.

7697 buying of business- commissions: The buying, after a death or while a death is impending, of funeral directing and embalming business by the licensee, the licensee's agents, assistants or employees, or the direct or indirect
payment, or offer of payment, of a commission by the licensee, the licensee's agents, assistants or employees for the purpose of such buying of business, constitutes a ground for disciplinary action.

7699 aiding, abetting unlicensed practitioner: Aiding or abetting an unlicensed person to practice funeral directing or embalming constitutes a ground for disciplinary action.

7700 prohibition of profane language: Using profane, indecent, or obscene language in the course of the preparation for burial, removal, or other disposition of, or during the funeral service for, human remains, or within the immediate hearing of the family or relatives of a deceased, whose remains have not yet been interred or otherwise disposed of constitutes a ground for disciplinary action.

7701, 7701.5 acceptance of kickbacks: Solicitation or acceptance by a licensee of any commission or bonus or rebate in consideration of recommending or causing human remains to be disposed of in any crematory, mausoleum or cemetery constitutes a ground for disciplinary action.

7702 use of previously used caskets: Using any casket or part of a casket which has previously been used as a receptacle for, or in connection with the burial or other disposition of, human remains constitutes a ground for disciplinary action; provided, however, this section shall not apply to exterior casket hardware which is not sold to the purchaser, or where same is reserved by contract.

7706 refusal to surrender dead body:
Refusing to surrender promptly the custody of human remains, the personal effects, and any certificate or permit required under Division 102 (commencing with Section 102100) of the Health and Safety Code that is in the possession or control of the licensee upon the express order of the person lawfully entitled to custody of the human remains constitutes a ground for disciplinary action.

7707 gross negligence: Gross negligence, gross incompetence or unprofessional conduct in the practice of funeral directing or embalming constitutes a ground for disciplinary action.

7716 paying money to secure business: Every funeral establishment, funeral director or embalmer, or
the agents or representatives thereof, who, after a death or while death is impending, pays, offers to pay or causes to be paid, directly or indirectly, any sum of money or other valuable consideration for the securing of business is guilty of a misdemeanor.

7718 soliciting or accepting money: Every person who, after a death or while a death is impending, solicits or accepts any sum of money or other valuable consideration, directly or indirectly, from a funeral establishment, funeral director or embalmer, his, her, or its agent or representative, in order that the funeral establishment, funeral director or embalmer might obtain business, is guilty of a misdemeanor.

7718.5 unlicensed person as fd: Every person as an individual, as a partner in a partnership or as an officer or employee of a corporation, association or other organization, who, without a license, holds himself or herself out as a funeral director, is guilty of a misdemeanor.

7735 required holding in trust of money: No funeral establishment licensed under the laws of the State of California, or the agents or employees of a funeral establishment, shall enter into or solicit any preneed arrangement, contract, or plan, hereinafter referred to as "contract," requiring the payment to the licensee of money.

7737.3 commingled preneed trust funds: All commingled preneed trust funds held by a funeral establishment shall be subject to an annual, independent certified financial audit with a copy of the audit to be submitted to the bureau for review within 120 days of the close of the fund's fiscal
year.

7737.5 deposit in federally insured association: A trustee may deposit the corpus of the trust in any financial institution insured by the Federal Deposit Insurance Corporation.

7737.7 trust corpus deposit in credit union: A trustee may deposit the corpus of the trust in any credit union which is insured by the National Credit Union Share Insurance

7738 right of FD to deposit money for endowment care: A licensed funeral establishment that is also a licensed cemetery authority shall not deposit any money or securities received in connection with preneed funeral arrangements in a special endowment care fund as provided in Article 4.

7741 inapplicability of article: Nothing in this article shall apply to cemetery property; cemetery commodities; cemetery service; or merchandise that is delivered as soon as paid for.

5217 formaldehyde: Action level. Action level means a concentration of 0.5 part formaldehyde per million parts of air (0.5 ppm) calculated as an eight (8)-hour time weighted average (TWA) concentration.

1209 ambulance, hearses, and first call cars: All ambulances, hearses and first-call or pickup cars and the equipment therein shall be kept clean and sanitary and free from deleterious odors at all times.

1214 authorization for dispose with and without embalming: Except as otherwise provided in Health and Safety Code Section 7304, human remains shall not be embalmed without the express authorization of a person having the legal right to control disposition of the remains. Such authorization shall be secured by use of the form prescribed by the bureau, attached hereto as Exhibit 1, and made a part of this regulation.

1215 attire while embalming: Every person, while engaged in actually embalming human remains, shall be attired in a clean and sanitary smock or gown covering the person from neck to below the knees, and shall, while so engaged, wear impervious gloves; and the body being embalmed shall at all times be so covered as to insure the privacy of said body.

1222 embalming fluids: No embalming fluids shall be used in embalming which contain heavy minerals or metallic substances which have a poisonous effect, such as arsenic, lead and mercury.

Funeral Director Examination Florida

Alternative Container: Unfinished wood box or other nonmetal receptacle or enclosure, without ornamentation or a fixed interior lining, that is designed for the encasement of human remains and that is made of fiberboard, pressed wood, composition materials, or like material.

At-Need Solicitation: Any uninvited contact by a licensee or his or her agent for the purpose of the sale of burial services or merchandise to the family or next of kin of a person after his or her death has occurred.

Below ground crypts: Interment space in preplaced chambers, either side by side or multiple depth covered by earth and sod and known also as "lawn crypts," "Westminster's." or "turf-top crypts".

Funeral goods/burial merchandise: Any personal property offered or sold by any person for use in connection with the final disposition, memorialization, interment, entombment, or inurnment of human remains or cremated remains.

Burial right: The term which means the right to use a grave space, mausoleum, columbarium, ossuary, or scattering garden for the interment, entombment, inurnment, or other disposition of human remains or cremated remains.

Funeral Service: Any service offered or provided in connection with the final disposition, memorialization, interment, entombment, or inurnment of human remains or cremated remains.

Care and maintenance: Perpetual process of keeping a cemetery and its lots, graves, grounds, landscaping, roads, paths, etc. in a well-cared-for and dignified condition.

Casket: A rigid container that is designed for the encasement of human remains and that is usually constructed of wood or metal, ornamented, and lined with fabric.

Cemetery: A place dedicated to and used or intended to be used for the permanent interment of human remains or cremated remains.

Cemetery Company: Any legal entity that owns or controls cemetery lands or property.

Centralized embalming facility: A facility in which embalming takes place that operates independently of a funeral establishment licensee and that offers embalming services to funeral directors for a fee.

Bank of below ground crypts: Any construction unit of below ground crypts that is acceptable to the Department of Financial Services and that a cemetery uses to initiate its below ground crypt program or to add to existing below ground crypt structures.

Cinerator: A facility where dead human bodies are subjected to cremation.

Closed container: Any container in which cremated remains can be placed and closed in a manner so as to prevent leakage or spillage of the remains.

Columbarium: A structure of building that is substantially exposed above the ground and that is intended to be used for the inurnment of cremated remains.

Common business enterprise: A group of two or more business entities that share common ownership in excess of 50 percent.

Cremated remains: All the remains of the human body recovered after the completing of the cremation process, including processing or pulverization that leaves only bone fragments reduced to unidentifiable dimensions and may include the residue of any foreign matter, including the residue of any foreign matter, including casket material, bridgework, or eyeglasses that were cremated with the human remains.

Cremation: Any mechanical or thermal process whereby a dead human body is reduced to ashes and bone fragments. Also includes any other mechanical or thermal process whereby human remains are pulverized, burned, re-cremated, or otherwise further reduced in size or quantity.

Cremation chamber: Enclosed space within which the cremation process takes place. Anything covered by these procedures shall be used exclusively for the cremation of human remains.

Cremation container: The casket or alternative in which the human remains are transported to and placed in the cremation chamber for a cremation.

Cremation interment container: A rigid outer container, that, subject to a cemetery's rules and regulations, is composed of concrete, steel, fiberglass, or some similar material in which an urn is placed prior to being interred in the ground and that is designed to support the earth above the urn.

Board of funeral, cemetery, and consumer services: What Florida department oversees the Funeral Services issues.

Direct disposal establishment: A facility licensed under chapter 382 where a direct disposer practices direct disposition.

Licensee: Any person licensed under chapter 382 to practice direct disposition in Florida.

Disinterment: The removal of a dead body from earth interment or aboveground interment.

Embalmier: Any person licensed under chapter 382 to practice embalming in Florida

Final Disposition: The final disposition of a dead human body by earth interment, above ground interment, cremation, burial at sea, or delivery to a medical institution for lawful dissection if the medical institution assumes responsibility for disposal.

Funeral Service: The observances, services, or ceremonies held to commemorate the life of a specific deceased human being at which time the remains are present.

Funeral director: Any person licensed under chapter 382 to practice funeral directing in Florida.

Funeral Home: A facility licensed under chapter 382 where a funeral director or embalmer practices funeral directing or embalming.

Grave space: A space of ground in a cemetery intended to be used for the interment in the ground of human remains.

Human remains: The body of a deceased human person for which a death certificate or fetal death certificate is required under chapter 382 and includes the body in any stage of decomposition.

Mausoleum: A structure or building that is substantially exposed above the ground and that is intended to be used for the entombment of human remains.

Monument: Any product used for identifying a grave site and cemetery memorials of all types, including monuments, markers, and vases.

Monument establishment: A facility that operates independently of a cemetery or funeral establishment and that offers to sell monuments or monument services to the public placement in a cemetery.

Niche: A compartment or cubicle for the memorialization or permanent placement of a container or urn containing cremated remains.

Ossuary: A receptacle used for the communal placement of cremated remains without benefit of any urn or any other container in which cremated remains may be commingled with other cremated remains and are non-recoverable.

Outer burial container: An enclosure into which a casket is placed and includes, but is not limited to, vaults made out of concrete, steel, fiberglass, or copper; sectional concrete enclosures; crypts; and wooded enclosure.

Personal residence: Any residential building in which one temporarily or permanently maintains his or her abode.

Practice of funeral directing: The performance by a licensed funeral director of any functions authorized by s. 497.372.

Pre-need contract: Any arrangement or method, of which the provider of funeral merchandise or services has actual knowledge, whereby any person agrees to furnish funeral merchandise or service in the future.

Preneed sales agent: Any person who is licensed under chapter 487 to sell preneed burial or funeral service and merchandise contracts or direct disposition contracts in Florida.

Processing: The reduction of identifiable bone fragments after the completion of the cremation and processing to unidentifiable bone fragments by manual means.

Pulverization: The reduction of identifiable bone fragments after the completion of the cremation and processing to granulated particles by manual or mechanical means.

Refrigeration facility: A facility that is operated independently of a funeral establishment, crematory, or direct disposal establishment that maintains space and equipment for the storage and refrigeration of dead human bodies.

Removal services: Any service that operates independently of a funeral establishment or a direct disposal that handles the initial removal of dead human bodies, and that offers its service to funeral establishments and direct disposal establishments for a fee.

Scattering garden: A location set aside, within a cemetery, that is used for the spreading of broadcasting of cremated remain that have been removed from their container and can be mixed with or placed on top of the soil or ground cover or buried in an underground receptacle on a commingled basis and that are non-recoverable.

Solicitation: Any communication that directly or implicitly requests an immediate oral response from the recipient.

Temporary container: A receptacle for cremated remains usually made of cardboard, plastic, or similar material designated to hold the cremated remains until an urn or other permanent container is acquired.

Urn: A receptacle designed to permanently encase cremated remains.

Pennsylvania Funeral Director/Embalmer Exam

Student Trainee:

* 2 years of college/liberal arts (or integrated course of study)
*accepted for matriculation at a mortuary college or university

Resident Intern

training in a funeral establishment in the Commonwealth under the supervision of a qualified preceptor

Preceptor

licensed and qualified funeral director in good standing with the Board may supervise 1 intern for every 35 funerals completed in the year before the request.

By accepting position a FD is required to fulfill duties set out by board, otherwise may result in suspension or revocation of license

Restriction of Intern

May not have other employment or attend school that interferes with training

Preceptor Instruction

*Laws of the Commonwealth pertaining to the profession

*The complete theory of FD services:

- Initial call details

- embalming

- cosmetizing of bodies

- dressing of bodies

- directing funerals

- selling of funeral service merchandise

- recordkeeping

- purchasing of necessary supplies

- preparing death certificates and documents

- preparing applications for certain death benefits

- follow up with family

- counseling of family

- instruction in prepaid burial accounts

- professional responsibilities

Notification of discontinuance

FD and intern must notify board of discontinuance

Interruption of internship for 30 days or more will require resident intern training to begin anew

Length of training

resident intern shall complete 12 full continuous months and shall work a minimum of 40 hours a week

Minimum cases

During training intern shall complete detail relating to instruction on a minimum of 35 deceased individuals 1 year of age or older under preceptor and must maintain case history

Complete funeral transactions

intern shall be present at at least 35 complete funeral transactions from initial call to internment and follow up

Affidavit of preceptor

Preceptor must submit affidavit of 35 cases intern has completed

a preceptor who falsifies an affidavit may, after due notice and hearing, be subject to licensure revocation or suspension for a period of time determined by the board

preceptor who refuses to furnish affidavit must submit to Board a reason for refusal

Examination requirements

National Board Examination

Written and oral examination by the authorized by the Bureau

Limited License

A person licensed by a reciprocal state to practice the profession of funeral director shall apply to the Board including:

Original certification from reciprocal state

Fee prescribed

Subject to biennial renewal

Shall become inactive upon the revocation, suspension, placement upon inactive status or other lapse of holder's license in the reciprocal state. Board may reinstate to active status upon proof that the holder's license in the reciprocal state is no longer revoked.

Board may take disciplinary action against the holder of a limited license for unprofessional conduct in the Commonwealth.

Licensure designations

Each FD license shall designate the name of the licensee and a place where the licensee may practice

A FD may practice only at an establishment designated in the director's license to practice funeral directing unless the FD also has a branch office license

Use of name of predecessor

A sole proprietorship or partnership may be conducted under the name of a predecessor funeral establishment if the name of the owner or partners appear as operator on all signs, form and advertising

Approval of funeral establishment

Person applying for approval from the Board to own or operate a funeral establishment, branch funeral establishment, partnership, or corporation shall submit necessary applications of forms provided.

Must include required fee, statement of applicant of right to occupy premises, letterhead, statement of funeral goods and svc for at need and preneed, a telephone listing and an inspection report

Submit withing 30 days of settlement, written notification that prepaid burial contracts have been transferred

Requirements for funeral establishments

Preparation room for preparation of human remains

Proper area or room for reposing of remains

Restroom facilities

Shared physical establishment

2 or more FDs may conduct separate businesses at the same physical establishment if each business separately maintains its own books, records, advertising,

signs and all other types and kinds of business operation, subject to Board approval

Licensees shall give 60 days advance notice of intention to the Board, accompanied by certified copy of the agreement. Changes shall be reported to the Board

Partnership license

Partnerships shall be licensed. A license will be issued in the names of the licensed partners as specific in the agreement. *A copy of the agreement* shall accompany the application fr the license as well as address of principal place of business.

Changes shall be reported to the board within 30 days

Branch license

Application shall be submitted with necessary forms for approval

Shall have same facilities as principal place of business

Each branch shall have a currently licensed FD in good standing assigned as Supervisor

Licensed FD acting as supervisor may do embalmings and funeral directing part time for other establishments if it does not interfere with duties

Letterheads, statements of funeral goods and services etc, shall show name and address of principal place, address of branch and name of supervisor

Termination of branch license

License terminates with the discontinuance of the principal place of business

Widow, widower and estate licenses

Upon death of licensee, Board will issue a license and renewal to the estate of the deceased for a period not to exceed 3 years, or to the widow or widower of the deceased without time limitation, if the widow or widower remains unmarried and has written notice of intent to continue practice

Must inform board within 10 days of deceased's death and request application

License should be filed within 30 days of deceased's death. Widow/er must include death certificate and marriage certificate

Must lave licensed FD assigned as permanent supervisor

Temporary supervisor may be assigned for not more than 6 months

FH name shall remain the same, and must be at same location

Preparation room

Human remains must be completely prepared in preparation room of establishment, except for preautopsy embalming in an approved establishment

Room must be approved by the Board

Prep room facilities

Sink with running water and sewerage connections and possessing a 2 inch capacity drain pipe

metal or porcelain embalming table

metal cabinet or metal or glass shelves or a material impervious to water and stain

covered waste container

first aid kit

surgical instruments and non backflow type aspirator

airtight walls/ceiling

floor impervious to water

outside ventilation, may be screened widonw or 8 inch pipe leading to exterior of building

solid doors

sterilizer, chemical or otherwise

flushing facilities to flush corrosive materials including eye shower, clean cold water, portable eye washers approved by OSHA

Rubber gloves

Goggles

PPE

FD General knowledge

FD is responsible for the knowledge of and compliance with State and local health laws and regulations , including OSHA regulations

Food and beverage

Food may not be served to the public in any part of a funeral establishment. Nonalcoholic beverages may be served in an area approved by the Board. Proper sanitation must be maintained.

Prompt disposal of deceased body

May not allow retention of a dead human body for a total of more than *10 days* without special permission from the board

New establishments

must receive Board inspection before commencing operation

Use of prep room

Prep room must be used only for embalming human remains. Equipment or supplies not used for embalming must not be stored in prep room. Bodies must be prepared in consort with religious beliefs of family.

Embalming or preparation of body

only a currently licensed FD or registered resident intern with supervision may prepare or embalm body. Only authorized staff may be permitted in the prep room

Advertising

FD must not make inaccurate or deceptive statements, representation, guaranty, warranty, testimonial or endorsement

Names used in advertising must be living, licensed individuals. Deceased licensed family members can be used if noted "deceased."

Prices may not be announced that give impression that they include services or merchandise which FD noes not intend to supply

Professional responsibilities of FD

Full and factual representation of services rendered of products provided

counseling of family in selection of services and furnishings

Confidentiality of information

acquainting of religious practices

releasing remains to FD chosen by family

Proper disposal of human remains

remains held 24 hours beyond death shall be embalmed or sealed , or kept under refrigeration refrigerated remains over 24 hours beyond death shall be kept between 35 and 40 degrees F. Remains shall be buried, cremated or entombed within 5 hours of removal from refrigeration

Public should not view an unembalmed body kept in refrigeration over 36 hours

Family must provide written authorization of who is to be cremated

Unprofessional conduct

Aiding or assisting a FD whose license has been suspended or revoked, or unlicensed person engaging in act or practice which requires license

Disrespect or mutilation of remains

Defaming another FD publicly

Participating in business or professional relationship whose scheme or plan interferes with rights of person entitled to dispose of body

Paying commission for solicitation of clientele

Offering money or item of value to influence employee of the Commonwealth

Failing to notify Bureau in writing for demand or extortion of money on behalf of employee of commonwealth

Attempting to influence judgement of family

Aiding or abetting another licensed FD to violate act

Furnishing embalming w/o written permission

Renting funeral establishment for the purpose of creating a secondary location (renting over 10 times a year)

performing services on behalf of entity that is not in compliance

Refusing to release remains without consideration, earned or not

Failing to comply w/FTC funeral rule

Cremation

Dead human body may be cremated any time after 24 hours beyond time of death. Body may be taken to the crematory before that with written instruction.

Transportation

Body must be transported face up, horizontally, and covered so it is shielded from public view

Commercial transport costs must be explained to family

Supervision of funeral service and internment

FD must personally supervise funeral service at cemetery and have a representative present until deceased is interred.

License renewal

Biennially. Expires 1st of February in even years.

Active duty FD's

Notify board within 10 days of military orders

If supervisor, FH has *30 days to notify board and have "temporary supervisor"*

Continuing Education

During each biennial renewal, licensed FD must complete 6 hours of continuing ed

Unclaimed bodies shipped by cc

Bodies which remain unclaimed for *36 hours after death* shall fall under the jurisdiction of the Human Gifts Registry and shipped in accordance with its procedures

Certificates and Cause of Death

The coroner shall issue a certificate of cause of death in all cases referred to him by the local registrar of vital statistics

Shipped bodies

Except for bodies shipped by air, embalmed bodies shall be shipped by placing the casket in a box of strong lumber not less than 7/8 inch thick, bearing at least 4 carrying handles, 2 on each side, or six when the box is over 5'6"

Disinterment

No dead body shall be removed from its place if interment unless a disinterment permit is first obtained.

1. Funeral director or cemetery official must present to the local registrar the correct name, date and cause of death and written consent of next of kin

2. No disinterred body shall be reinterred within the commonwealth unless a burial permit is obtained

3. Disinterment permits are void *after 72 hours* from date of issue. No disinterment between sunset and sunrise

4. Disinterment permits must be delivered to sexton or other person in charge of the cemetery and shall be returned to the registrar *within 30 days*

Transportation of disinterred body

Forbidden with common carrier unless in hermetically sealed container. certification is required. Registrar must issue permit

Exhumation and exposure

Remains must not be exposed to view without an order of a court

Crypt

Crypt must be fitted with durable covering which may be tightly sealed unless remains are in a sealed container

Mausoleum

Remains must be in Sealed container

Transit permit

In addition to burial permit with bodies being shipped by cc, transit permit must be securely attached to the shipping container

Depth of outer case (vault)

The distance of the top of the outer case (vault) containing the casket may be not less than 1.5 feet (18 inches) from the natural surface of the ground

Depth of casket/body

When a casket is not placed in an outer case or when a body is not placed in a casket, the distance from parts of the body or casket may be no less than 2 feet (24 inches) from the natural surface of the ground

Receiving vaults

Receiving vaults may be used for the temporary reception of dead bodies if the bodies are properly embalmed for a period *not exceeding 30 days,* beyond which special permission from the Department of Health is required. The responsible person in charge of the body may make a request for special permission at least one week before the expiration of the 30 day period.

Receiving vault burial permit

A new burial permit must be secured by the person responsible beyond the 30 day period

Death certificate

Must be filed within *96 hours of death*

WIDOW'S LICENSE: Board will issue a license and renewal to the estate of the deceased for a period not to exceed...

not to exceed 3 years, or to the widow or widower of the deceased WITHOUT TIME LIMITATION if the widow or widower remains unmarried and has written notice of intent to continue practice

When a licensee dies...

Estate/widow must inform board within 10 days of deceased's death and request application

License should be filed within *30 days of deceased's death.** Widow/er must include death certificate and marriage certificate

Widow licensee and supervisor

Must lave licensed FD assigned as permanent supervisor

Temporary supervisor may be assigned for **not more than 6 months**

Refrigerated remains

Remains held 24 hours beyond death shall be embalmed or sealed , or kept under refrigeration

refrigerated remains over 24 hours beyond death shall be kept between **35 and 40 degrees F**. Remains shall be buried, cremated or entombed within 5 hours of removal from refrigeration

Public should not view an unembalmed body kept in refrigeration over...

36 hours

10 days

*estate/widow must inform of licensee death within 10 days

*active duty must notify board within 10 days of military orders

*FH must not keep body for more than 10 days without special permission from board

30 days

- widow/estate license must be filed within 30 days of licensees death

-active duty must notify board and elect a temporary supervisor within 30 days

- receiving vaults may be used not to exceed 30 days

-interruption of internship for more than 30 days will require resident to begin training anew

- change of partnership must be reported to board within 30 days

-opening new funeral establishment : Submit within 30 days of settlement, written notification that prepaid burial contracts have been transferred

-Disinterment permits must be delivered to sexton or other person in charge of the cemetery and shall be returned to the registrar within 30 days

-temporary supervisor for widow's licensee business is permitted for 30 days if permanent supervisor has left, retired, etc.

60 days

shared physical establishment: Licensees shall give 60 days advance notice of intention to the Board, accompanied by certified copy of the agreement.

5 hours

remains must be interred or cremated within 5 hours of removal from refrigeration

6 hours

continuing ed for each biennial period

24 hours

- bodies held over 24 hours must be embalmed or refrigerated

- Cremation must wait until 24 hours after death

36 hours

-bodies unclaimed fall under jurisdiction of human gifts registry

-Public should not view unembalmed body after 36 hours of refrigeration

6 months

maximum time a temporary supervisor at a widow's licensee business is permitted

48 hours

Written report of child abuse must be submitted within 48 hours of oral report (which should be reported immediately on ChildLine)

Ohio Funeral Director/Embalmer Exam

Acknowledgment Cards

Cards of recognition sent to friends for kindness shown to a deceased's family.

Acolyte

An alter attendant.

Adaptive Funeral Rite

A funeral rite that is adjusted to the needs and wants of those directly involved; one which has been altered to suit the trends of the times.

Aftercare (Post -Funeral Follow-Up)

Those appropriate and helpful acts of counseling that come after the funeral.

Allah

In the Islam faith, the name of God.

Altar

An elevated place of or structure on which sacrifices are offered or at which religious rites are performed; in the Christian faith, a table on which the Eucharist or Holy Communion is offered.

Alternative Container

An unfinished wood box or other non-metal receptacle or enclosure, without ornamentation or a fixed interior lining, which is designed for the encasement of human remains and which is made of fiberboard , pressed-wood, composition materials (with or without an outside covering) or like materials.

Apostille

Certification/legalization of a document for international use; under terms of the 1961 Hague Convention.

Archbishop

In the Roman Catholic faith, the head of an archdiocese.

Aron

Hebrew word meaning container; a casket made entirely of wood, containing no metal parts.

Arrangements Conference

The meeting between the funeral director and the client family during which the funeral arrangements are discussed.

Artificial Grass

An imitation of grass made in mat form and used at the cemetery to cover the earth around the grave.

At-Need Counseling

Counseling with the family as they select the services and items of merchandise in completing arrangements for the funeral service of their choice when a death has occurred.

Bishop

Leader of multiple churches in a particular denomination; in the Roman Catholic faith, the head of a diocese; in the LDS (Mormon) church, Bishop of the ward is leader of a single church.

Bonze

The name of the Buddhist priest.

Book of Dates

A term used in the Buddhist faith to describe a calendar that is used to determine an accurate time for casketing the body.

Brother

In the Roman Catholic faith, a man who is a member of a religious order without being ordained or while preparing for ordination.

Brotherhood

Relating to a social organization.

Burial-Trasit Permit (Disposition Permit)

A legal document, issued by a governmental agency, authorizing transportation and/or disposition of a dead human body.

Canopy (Cemetery Tent)

A portable shelter used to cover the grave area during the committal.

Cantor

A religious singer who assists the clergy; assists the Rabbi in the Jewish faith; assists the Priest in the Eastern Orthodox faith.

Cardinal

In the Roman Catholic faith, a dignity conferred upon Bishops making them Princes of the Church.

Cash advance

Cash advance items may include, but are not limited to: Cemetery or Crematory Services, Paul bearer's, public transportation, clergy honoraria, flowers, musicians or singers, nurses, obituary notices, gratuities, and death certificates; sometimes called an accommodation or cash disbursement.

Casket Bearer (Pallbearer)

One who actively Bears or carries the casket during the funeral service and at the committal service.

Celebrant

The efficient who celebrates the mass and the Roman Catholic Church.

Cemetery

An area of the ground set aside and dedicated for the final disposition of dead human bodies.

Certified copy of a death certificate

A legal copy of the original death certificate.

Chancel

The portion of the church surrounding the altar, usually in closing the clergy; area behind the altar or communion rail.

Chapel

A building or designated area of a building in which the services are conducted

Chaplin

A person chosen to conduct religious exercises for the military, the chapel of an institution or fraternal organization.

Chevrah Kadisha

Hebrew phrase meaning "Holy Society," a group of men or women from the synagogue who care for the dead; they may be referred to by laymen as the "washers."

Christian Burial Certificate

A letter or form from a priest stating the eligibility of the deceased for burial in a Roman Catholic Cemetery

Columbarium

A structure, room, or space in a mausoleum or other building containing niches or recesses used to hold cremated remains.

Committal service

The portion of the funeral that is conducted at the place of disposition of dead human bodies.

Common carrier

Any carrier required by law to convey passengers or freight without refusal if the approved fare or charge is paid (airline, train, etc.).

Contemporary funeral Rite

Funeral observances that reflect present day (modern) influences in lieu of (or in addition to or as part of) the traditional ceremonies.

Corner

A public officer whose Chief duty is to investigate questionable deaths. (also see: medical examiner)

Cortege

Historical reference for funeral procession.

Cot

A portable stretcher commonly employed in an ambulance or transfer vehicle for the moving of the sick comma injured, or deceased.

Cremated remains

The result of the reduction of a dead body to inorganic bone fragments by intense heat in a specially designed retort.

Crematory (Crematorium)

A furnace or retort for cremating dead human bodies; a building that houses a retort.

Cross

The religious emblem consisting of two plain bars that intersect at right angles to each other.

Crucifier/Crossbearer

One who carries the crucifix/cross during an ecclesiastical procession.

Crucifix

A cross with a figure or image representing the body of Christ (Corpus) on it.

Crypt

A chamber in a mausoleum, generally used to contain the casket and remains of a deceased person.

Deacon

A subordinate officer in a Christian Church.

Death certificate

A legal document containing Vital Statistics, disposition, and final medical information pertaining to the deceased.

Death notice

A classified notice publicizing the death of a person and giving those details of the funeral service that the survivors wish to have published.

Deceased

A dead human body.

Dentures

False teeth.

Department of Veterans Affairs or VA

(previously known as Veterans Administration)

A federal agency that administers benefits provided by law for the veterans of the Armed Forces.

Diocese

In the Roman Catholic faith, a geographical grouping of parishes under the jurisdiction of a bishop.

Direct cremation

Disposition of human remains by cremation, without formal viewing, visitation or ceremony with body present. [16 CFR 453 (g)]

Direct disposition

Any method of disposition of the human remains without photo viewing, visitation or ceremony with the body present.

Dismissal

Leading to an organized departure or inviting to leave.

Divine Liturgy

Liturgical celebration of the Eucharist in Eastern Orthodox churches.

Ecclesiastic

Pertaining to church or clergy.

Elegy

Song or poem expressing sorrow or lamentation for the Dead.

Elder

In the Jehovah's Witness faith, the person who typically conduct the service.

El Male Rachamin

In the Jewish faith, a memorial service; literally "God full of compassion;" usually the last prayer of the funeral service: sometimes referred to as the Malei.

Entombment

The placing of remains in a crypt or mausoleum.

Epitaph

A commemorative inscription on a tomb or cemetery marker.

Escort

To accompany, as a leader of the procession or guardian of the group; military personnel assigned to accompany a body following an active-duty death.

Eucharistic

The consecrated elements of Holy Communion.

Eucharistic minister

Layperson sanctioned to administer Holy Communion and other assigned tasks.

Eulogy

An oration praising an individual, usually after death.

Event planning

Process of planning and / or coordinating a ceremony or activity.

Final Commendation

In the Roman Catholic faith, the ending portion of the funeral mass.

Forwarding remains

One of the categories required to be itemized on the GPL. This involves the service of the funeral provider in the locale where death occurs in preparation for transfer to another Funeral provider as selected by the family

Fraternal

Relating to a social organization

Funeral service

The rites held at the time of disposition of human remains, with the body present.

Funeral arrangements

The term applied to the completing of the service and financial details of the funeral at the time of need.

Funeral liturgy (Funeral Mass)

The name of the funeral service in the Roman Catholic Church.

Funeral procession

The procession of vehicles from the place of the funeral to the place of disposition.

Funeral rites

Any funeral event perform in a solemn and prescribed manner.

Funeral service

The rights held at the time of disposition of human remains, with the body present.

Gatha

The first two and last two verses of a Buddhist hymn song at the funeral service.

General price list (GPL)

A printed list of goods and services offered for sale by funeral provider with retail prices. GPL is considered the Keystone of the funeral right.

Genuflect

The act of bending the knee as an indication of reverence or as an act of humility.

Gratuity (Tip)

Gift or small sum of money tendered for a service provided.

Grave

An excavation in the Earth has a place for interment

Graveside service

A funeral service, religious or otherwise, conducted at the grave.

Grave straps

Webbing or similar material used for lowering the casket into the grave.

"Green"

Ecologically friendly.

Guaranteed contract

One where the funeral home guarantees that the services and merchandise will be provided at the time of need for an amount not exceeding the original amount of the contract plus any accruals, regardless of the cost of providing the services and merchandise at the time of the funeral

Hesped

In the Jewish faith, a eulogy or true evaluation of the deceased life that is part of the funeral service.

Holy water

Water blessed by a priest.

Honorarium (Plural: Honoraria; Honorariums)

A nominal compensation or recognition for service performed.

Honorary pallbearers

Friends of the family or members of an organization or group who act as an escort or honor guard for the deceased. They do not carry the casket.

Humanist funeral

A funeral right that is in essence devoid of religious connotation.

Icon

In the Eastern Orthodox Faith, a holy picture; usually Mosaic or painted on wood.

Iconostasis (Iconostas, Iconostation)

In the Eastern Orthodox Church, the partition that extends across the front of the church separating the sanctuary from the solea.

IHS

The first three letters in the Greek word for Jesus.

Imam

In the Islamic faith, the leader of the local congregation.

Immediate burial

Disposition of human remains by Burial, without formal viewing, visitation or ceremony with the body present, except for a graveside service. [16 CFR. 453.1 (k)]

Inter (Inhume)

To bury in the ground

Interment (Burial, Inhumement/Inhumation)

The act of placing the dead human body in the ground.

Inurnment

The act of placing cremains in an urn. (CANA definition) act of placing cremated remains in a niche or grave.

Irrevocable contract

Contract for future funeral services which cannot be terminated or cancelled prior to the death of the beneficiary.

Islam

The religion of Muslims (Moslems) that began at the time of Muhammad; Muslims believe that Islam stands for Purity, peace, submission to God's (Allah,s) Will, and obedience to his loss.

Jinazah

In the Islamic faith, the funeral or funeral prayer.

Kaddish

In the Jewish faith, a prayer recited for the deceased by the direct mourners (parents, siblings, spouse, and children) for the first time at the conclusion of internet service. It is subsequently recited by children for parents at every service for 11 months. All other categories of mourners have the obligation to say the Kaddish for 30 days.

Kever

In the Jewish faith, the grave.

Kevurah

In the Jewish faith, the burial.

Kin

One's relatives; referring to blood relationship (legally the surviving spouse is not can).

Kingdom Hall

The appropriate term for the worship facility for the Jehovah's Witnesses.

Koran (Quran)

A holy book of the Islamic faith, revealed to Muhammad by the angel Gabriel.

Kriah

Hebrew word meaning rendering or tearing; a symbol of grief; a tear in the upper corner of the Garment or a tear and a symbolic ribbon which is worn by the survivors.

Levaya

In the Jewish faith, the funeral procession.

Liturgical (Eucharistic-Centered) Worship

A prescribed order or form of worship specific to a particular denomination which will have the Eucharistic or Holy Communion as its central element.

Lot

A subdivision of a cemetery that consists of several grave or interment spaces.

Lowering device

Mechanical device used to lower a casket into the ground.

Makura-gyo

Traditionally, in the Buddhist Faith, a bedside prayer which may now be performed by the bonze just before funeral arrangements are made.

Mass

The liturgical celebration of the Eucharist in the Roman Catholic Church.

Mass Card (spiritual bouquet)

A document indicating the offering of a Mass for a specific intention.

Mausoleum

A building containing crypts and vaults for entombment.

Medical examiner

A forensically trained physician whose duty is to investigate questionable or unattended deaths (has replaced the corner in some states).

Memorial folder (service folder)

A pamphlet made available at the funeral service giving details about the deceased and the funeral arrangements.

Memorial Gathering

A scheduled assembly of family and friends following a death.

Memorial Park

A cemetery, or section of the cemetery, with only flush-to-the-ground markers.

Memorial service

Funeral rites with the body not present.

Menorah

In the Jewish faith, a candelabrum with a central stem bearing seven candles; it is the oldest symbol in Judaism.

Military escort

Military personnel assigned to accompany a body following an active-duty death.

Mogen David (Star of David)

In the Jewish faith, a hexagram formed by the combination of two triangles. May be called the Jewish star. It symbolizes a new hope for the Jewish people.

Mohammad (Muhammad) (PBUH)

A prophet of the Islamic religion born 571 and considered by Muslims to be God's last messenger, but not worshipped and not considered to be divine. Mohammad is just a man like Jesus and Adam. They are men like any other humans. Prophet Jesus had no father. Prophet Adam had no father or mother. To Muslims, God is one and the only creator.

Monsignor

An honorary title conferred upon a priest.

Mosque (Masjid)

The local church building; contains no icons, statues, symbols, used, chairs, or musical instruments.

Muslim (Moslem)

The name given to a member of the Islamic faith.

Narthex (Lobby, Vestibule, Foyer)

The entryway into the funeral home or church.

National Cemetery

A cemetery created and maintained under an act of Congress for burial of veterans of military service and their eligible family members.

Nave

The seating or Auditorium section of a church.

Niche

A recess or space in a columbarium used for the permanent placing of cremated remains.

Nirvana

The Buddhist fantasy idea of heavenly peace or pure land. They consider Buddha a God, but Buddha himself never said that he was God and stated that he was just a man trying to do good deeds.

Non-guaranteed contract

One in which the funeral home only agrees that the amount prepaid plus any accruals will be credited to the balance due. However, the price of the funeral will be whatever the current price is the services and merchandise at the time the death occurs.

Non liturgical (scripture centered) worship

A form or order of worship which has the scripture as its central element; the actual form or order of the worship service is left to the discretion of each individual church and /or minister.

Obituary

A news item concerning the death of a person which usually contains a biographical sketch.

Obsequies

Funeral rites or burial ceremonies.

Officiant

One who conducts a religious service or ceremony.

Outer burial container

Any container which is designed for placement in the grave around the casket including, but not limited to, containers commonly known as Burial Vaults, grave boxes, and Grave liners.

Pagoda or Temple

The Buddhist place of worship.

Pallbearer

One who actively Bears or carries the casket during the funeral service and at the end of the committal service.

Parastas (Great Panachida)

Visual service associated with Eastern Orthodox funeral.

Paschal Candle

In the Roman Catholic faith, a candle placed near the casket during the funeral mass that signifies the Everlasting Light of Christ.

Pastor

One having spiritual care over a number of people.

Perpetual care

An arrangement made by the cemetery whereby funds are set aside, the income for which is used to maintain the cemetery plot in definitely.

Pope

The head of the Roman Catholic church and the bishop of Rome.

Prayer card

A card with the name of the decedent and a prayer or verse, which may or may not include the dates of birth and death.

Pre-funded funeral arrangements

Those funeral arrangements made in advance of need that include provisions for funding or prepayment.

Preplanned funeral arrangements

Those funeral arrangements made in advance of need that do not include Provisions for funding or prepayment.

Prie Dieu (prayer rail, kneeler)

A kneeling rail.

Georgia / Ohio Funeral Service Exam

How many members are on the SBOFS?

Seven

How is the SBOFS comprised?

Seven Members who are Appointed by the Governor. Six are funeral directors (five years experience in state), and one is a non-industry-consumer-advocate.

How long is the term for the SBOFS?

Six Years

How often does the SBOFS meet?

Required to meet annually, but meets monthly in Macon, GA.

What is the mission of the SBOFS?

Ensuring the proper care and disposition of dead human bodies.

The SBOFS is authorized to:

1. Develop standards of proficiency and qualifications for those engaged or wish to engage in FD/Emb.

2. Revoke and Suspend licenses.

3. Establish or amend the rules/regulations governing FD/Emb.

4. Develop standards of cleanliness and sanitation

5. Setting minimum standards of appearance for FH/Crematories

What is the role of the FDFCC?

Tasked with always making sure that the establishment is always in compliance with the regulations set forth by the SBOFS.

An FDFCC has ___ days to notify the SBOFS of separation from the establishment.

Five

An FDFCC has ___ days to notify the SBOFS of change of ownership of an establishment.

15

Can a person legally serve as the FDFCC for more than one establishment?

No

Georgia Cemetery & Funeral Services Act of 2000

Makes it unlawful for any person to offer or sell any preneed burial services or funeral merchandise in the state of Georgia without being registered as a preneed dealer or preneed agent.

Are preneed funds taxable?

No

100% of Preneed funds for burial/funeral expenses must be deposited in:

1. State Bank

2. State S&L

3. Federal Bank

4. Federal S&L

Preneed funds may NOT be:

1. Transferred

2. Pledged

3. Hypothecated

The preneed dealer shall have ___ days, after becoming aware of the fact, to correct any amount that is less than it should be.

15

Can interest from preneed funds be used by the FD to pay for merchandise?

No

Revocable Contract (Type of Preneed Contract)

May be terminated by the purchaser at any time prior to death with a refund of the monies paid.

Irrevocable Contract (Type of Preneed Contract)

The contract cannot be terminated or cancelled.

Guaranteed Contract (Type of Preneed Contract)

FH guarantees that the services and merchandise will be provided at the time of need for an amount not exceeding the original amount of the contract plus any interest.

Non-Guaranteed Contract (Type of Preneed Contract)

FH agrees that the amount prepaid plus any interest will be credited to the balance due. However, the cost of the funeral will be current pricing at the time of death.

Apprenticeship License

1. Must be registered with the SBOFS

2. Serve 3,120 hours in no less that 18 months

3. Regular business hours: 8am-10pm

4. Case/Hour reports should be submitted to the SBOFS every six months.

5. Apprenticeship must be served under a board approved supervising FD/Emb

6. Apprenticeship must be served at a board approved establishment.

How long must a preceptor be licensed before taking on an apprentice?

Three Years

FD/Emb License

1. Submit proper application to the SBOFS

2. Must be 18 years of age and have good character

3. High School Graduate or GED

4. Graduated from an accredited Mortuary College

5. Must have completed an apprenticeship of 3,120 hours (50 FD cases/50 Emb cases)

6. Pass a comprehensive exam of FD/Emb laws in the state of Georgia.

Establishment License (FH/Crematory)

1. Must be located at a specific street address and have the minimum facilities and equipment

2. 30-person capacity room used for conducting services.

3. Prep Room that has non-porous, sanitary floor & walls with proper ventilation & drainage.

4. Supplies and instruments needed for the preparation and embalming of human remains.

5. Must have a display room containing 8 caskets or mock-ups.

6. Must have one operable motor hearse and one set of church trucks.

Crematory License

1. Must have display room containing an adequate supply of urns.

2. Must have one operable retort for cremation.

Disciplinary Action by the SBOFS

1. The SBOFS is authorized to inspect all FH/Crematory establishments to insure compliance set forth by the SBOFS and Georgia law.

2. Inspections must take place at least one every calendar year.

3. The license of any establishment may be suspended, revoked or put on probation.

4. The SBOFS may levy fines if any rules or violations are noted upon inspection.

Who is responsible for completing and filing the Death Certificate?

Funeral Director

The death certificate must be filed with the local registrar in the county in which the death occurred within _____ days after death.

Ten

The Funeral Director who assumes custody of the deceased should file the death certificate within ___ hours.

72

The medical certification as to the cause of death should be completed, signed, and returned to the FD within ___ hours. (unless inquiry is required by the Georgia Death Investigation Act)

72

Death certificates are only issued to applicants who have a ___ and ___ interest-- primarily family members or legal representatives of the family.

Direct and Tangible

Who is authorized to request changes in writing to a previously filed death certificate?

1. State Registrar

2. Next of Kin

3. FD that embalmed the body

Burial/Transit Permit or Disposition Permit (Permit for the Disposition of Human Remains)

A legal document issued by the government agency that authorizes the FD to transport and/or dispose of human remains. It is the legal record that final disposition has occurred.

Is it a violation of the Amended Funeral Rule to embalm without permission?

NO, the violation of the rule occurs when a FD charges for the embalming performed without prior permission given.

Consequence of Embalming without permission

Can result in a Tort under state law in which the FD would be civilly liable.

Prior Permission to Embalm

Must be expressly given. May not be "permission to prepare the body".

Embalming without permission may occur if:

1. State Law requires it

2. Family gives permission (expressed or written)

3. Exigent Circumstances exist

Exigent Circumstances for Embalming Without Permission

1. Unable to contact family member or authorized person after exercising due dilligence.

2. FD has no reason to believe the family does not want embalming.

3. After embalming, FD informs family that if they choose a service that does not require embalming, no fee will be charged; but, if they choose a service that requires embalming a fee will be charged.

What is Due Diligence?

A FD must exhaust all means/methods known to contact the family without unduly delaying the embalming to preserve the body for possible services. Good practice to document the steps made in Due Diligence.

A person may be pronounced dead by:

1. Qualified Physician

2. Registered Professional Nurse

3. Qualified Physician Assistant

A Coroner, Deputy Coroner, or ME may make a pronouncement of death (in absence of the 3 medical professionals) if the following conditions are met:

1. Irreversible cessation of circulatory & respiratory functions

2. Irreversible cessation of all brain functions

The Coroner investigates when any person dies under the following circumstances:

1. Violence

2. Suicide or Casualty

3. Suddenly when in apparent good health

4. When unattended by a physician

5. Suspicious manner

6. Children from birth to 16 years of age

7. Death of inmates who die within 25 hours of being admitted to hospital

8. Foul Play

9. Accidental death

Use of Unclaimed Bodies

An unclaimed body can be made available for use, in this state only, for medical science purposes, upon review and approval of the SBOFS.

Pronouncement of a Hospice Patient Death

A RN licensed in the state of Georgia employed by the Hospice at the time of death and in the absence of a physician may make the determination and pronouncement of death.

Hospice Patient Death Organ Donor

When a Hospice patient is a registered organ donor, only a physician may make the determination and pronouncement of death.

Next of Kin Sequence

1. Healthcare Agent

2. Who is Warranted

3. Spouse

4. Adult Children

5. Parents

6. Siblings

Funeral Procession

Any array of vehicles were the lead vehicle displays a sign, flag, or insignia furnished by a funeral home indicating a funeral procession unless they are led by law enforcement and each vehicle in the procession is operating headlights. (OCGA 40-6-76 (2010)

Funeral Procession: Passing

Operators NOT in a funeral procession shall not pass the funeral procession on a 2 lane road-- results in $100 fine & misdemeanor charge.

Social Security Death Benefit

$255 payable to spouse or child

How many working credits do you need to qualify for Social Security Benefits?

40, 20 of which must be earned in the last ten years of employment.

VA Death Benefit $150

$150 interment/plot allowance for honorable veterans buried in a non-Federal cemetery who are eligible for the burial/funeral expense allowance.

VA Death Benefit $300

$300 burial/funeral expense allowance for veterans who at the time of their death were entitled to disability pension or compensation.

VA Death Benefit $1,500

$1,500 Benefit for veterans who die of a service connected disability in lieu of other burial/funeral benefits.

VA Death Benefits Allowable Items

1. Casket

2. Vault

3. Embalm

4. Organist

5. Hearse

6. Funeral Services

VA Death Benefits Non-Allowable Items

1. Flowers

2. Flower Car

3. Death Notices

4. Sales Tax

VA Form 21-530

Government Form used to file for VA Death Benefit Claims

Time frame to File VA Death Benefits for a Service Related Death

There is no time frame limitations for filing a claim for a Service Related Death.

VA Death Benefits Non-Service Related Deaths

Claim must be filed within two years of the Veteran's burial.

Deposits of Deceased Depositors

When a person dies intestate and has a bank account balance of $10,000 or less, the financial institution may pay proceeds to the surviving NOK. If no one claims the proceeds within 90 days, the financial institution is authorized to pay no more than $10,000 for funeral expenses.

Record Retention: GPL

One year from the date it was last distributed

Record Retention: Vital Records, Funeral Contracts, Payroll

Three Years

Record Retention: Training Records

Five Years

Record Retention: HR

Six Years

Record Retention: OSHA Injury/Illness

30 Years

Penalty for Disinterment without a proper permit

Disinterment without a proper permit is grounds for a misdemeanor.

The minimal amount of formaldehyde required in a 16 oz. bottle?

10%

On a Funeral Contract, who is party to the first part?

Funeral Home

On a Funeral Contract, who is party to the second part?

Whoever signs the contract

Before a cadaver is transferred to a Mortuary College or Medical College, they must request a:

Burial/Transit Permit

The lawful right of the funeral director undertaking funeral arrangements is primarily derived from what two sources?

1. Those imposed by statutes

2. Funeral Contract

Insurance: Freedom of Choice

It is unlawful for any insurer or insurance company to enter into contracts with funeral homes or others which may limit or restrict freedom of choice in the open market. (OCGA 33-1-10)

Authorizing Agent

A person legally entitled to authorize the cremation of human remains. (OCGA 43-18-80)

Alternative Container

Any receptacle or enclosure which is of sufficient strength to be used to hold and to transport a dead human body

Final Disposition

The final disposal of a dead human body whether it is by, but not limited to, earth interment, above-ground interment, cremation, burial at sea, or delivery to a medical institution for lawful dissection if the medical institution assumes responsibility for disposal.

Funeral Merchandise

The goods that may only be sold or offered for sale by a funeral director working in a funeral establishment and includes, but is not limited to, a casket or alternative container, but does not include an outer burial container or cemetery marker.

Funeral Service Contract

A written or oral agreement between a funeral director or funeral establishment and a legally authorized person for the embalming, funeral, or final disposition of a dead human body.

Outer Burial Container (OBC)

An enclosure into which a casket is placed, including, but not limited to, a vault made of concrete, steel, fiberglass, or copper, a sectional concrete enclosure, a crypt, or a wooden enclosure.

Soliciting

The making of any uninvited contact with another person by a funeral director or by a funeral director's agent, assistant, employer, or employee for the purpose of the sale of funeral services or merchandise but shall not mean any advertising which is directed to the public in general.

Healthcare Agent

A person appointed by a declarant to act for and on behalf of the declarant to make decisions related to consent, refusal, or withdrawal of any type of health care and decisions related to autopsy, anatomical gifts, and final disposition of a declarant's body when a declarant is unable or chooses not to make health care decisions for himself or herself.

Waiting Period for Cessation of Rights

Any person who does not exercise his or her right of disposition within two days of notification of the death of decedent or within three days of decedent's death, whichever is earlier.

Dispute Regarding the Right of Disposition

A funeral home shall not be liable for refusing to accept the remains or to inter or otherwise dispose of the remains of the decedent or complete the arrangements for the final disposition of the remains until the funeral home receives a court order or other written agreement signed by the parties in the disagreement that decides the final disposition of the remains.

Information in Good Faith

Any person signing a funeral service agreement, cremation authorization form, or any other authorization for disposition shall be deemed to warrant the truthfulness of any facts set forth therein, including the identity of the decedent whose remains are to be buried, cremated, or otherwise disposed of, and the party's authority to order such disposition.

Proper Identification of Human Remains

Prior to the interment or cremation of such dead body, affix on the ankle or wrist of the deceased a tag of durable, non-corroding material permanently marked with the name of the deceased, the date of death, the social security number of the deceased, the county and state of death, and the serial number of any prosthesis removed from the dead body by the funeral establishment or crematory.

Who may receive cremated remains from the crematory?

A crematory may deliver or release cremated remains to a funeral establishment or a legally authorized person.

Made in the USA
Las Vegas, NV
07 August 2024

93467147R00132